W9-BNN-075

Men, Children and Grass Farming

A Suburban Life

Joyce Fetzer Schutten

Judson Books

First Printing 2009

Orders: www.judsonbooks.com

Some of the pieces have been previously published in whole or in part.
Publications and publication dates are given in the Notes section.

LIBRARY OF CONGRESS CATALOGUING-IN-PUBLICATION DATA

Men, children and grass farming a suburban life: a collection of
personal essays by Joyce Fetzer Schutten

ISBN 978-1-60743-418-4

Library of Congress Control Number: 2009925777

Printed in the United States of America

For Lila

Contents

Jeremy at Bat

"Stee—riii—ek!!" The umpire has an emphatic style, the type who fills the air—a void created when the satisfying crack of ball on bat is not there. A chorus goes up from the crowd: "Good cut, Jeremy!" "That's okay!" "Come on, Jeremy, you can do it!"

Thing is, it wasn't a good cut. Jeremy had rested the bat on his neck and then swung it down to his ankles. I, a girl, could hit better when I was eight. But Jeremy plays on the Southwest Self Esteems and the parents don't want him to feel bad. Jeremy can't hit because he never plays baseball. The coach knows this so he schedules practices. I know this because I have a driver's license, and had to *drive* my sons to practice baseball.

I can remember back to my childhood, back when things were done right. In my town, Evanston, Illinois, there was no Little League that I ever heard of. This did-n't stop the neighborhood kids, mostly boys, from play-ing baseball. We lived next to a playground so I observed this firsthand. They played all the time. They broke windows. They broke our windows. Once a ball landed on the piano where I was practicing, and it was like an act of God, a snow day, because I *had* to stop. There was also glass all over the place and boys in hot water.

I don't remember seeing one dad in the playground. The fathers came home from work, took off their ties and had a highball with their wives, who had dinner ready. The dads were tired. They had won World War II and built the suburbs. They wanted a drink and the paper. Nothing interfered with dinner. Someone yelled at the kids, who stopped long enough to come in and have dinner.

The town I live in now, Bloomington, Minnesota, has baseball diamonds everywhere. Front yards are deco-rated with unused pitching nets, just as ours was. Never once in sixteen years have I driven by and seen kids playing a pick-up game of baseball. My guess is it's too adult driven. They like to ride dirt bikes and fool around with skateboards, build a fort in the ravine—activities that adults don't control. My son would get on the phone and organize as many kids as he could round up to play "Tree." This is a game of hide and seek or cops and robbers that had a different name every year. I had no idea what it was and that is probably why they liked it.

I'm concerned about the lack of baseball playing on

the part of kids in my town. Not that I like baseball. It makes me restless. It's the only sport that can have eight to ten seconds of dead air on TV. Live in the U.S. long enough and when you tune into dead air you know you're in the presence of baseball:

"So, two and 0's the count." (Seven seconds of dead air.) "You know, Bert, if they yank Slowey now and put in Perkins, that'll only be the third time since 1976 in the American League that they've switched out three pitchers in one inning who are lefties." Whose moms are in prison and have a horse named Jim. Where do they get this stuff? "You know, that's Mauer's twelfth cup adjustment and it's only the top of the fifth. If he goes another five, he'll be setting a personal record." Action. Stop action. Wait. Action. Stop action. Wait.

My father was raised in a small town in Indiana called North Liberty. During the innumerable and long trips there in his Ford Galaxy, my sister and I lounged around in the back seat in the blissful, death-defying days of no seat belts. Somehow she caught on. But I never did. I remained a baseball illiterate. Listening to Jack Brickhouse drone on and on was boring beyond belief. Also peaceful, secure, and just thinking about it reminds me of Lake Shore Drive, Stony Island and unscheduled summers. My dad often listened to two games at once. Maybe this is why batting averages never gave me goose bumps. I think this is when, however, I fell in love with the names. Like a conservative Catholic who loves the Latin Mass, I absorbed the litany of names, especially Latin American names. Just say, "Jose Canseco," and I feel soothed, snug. Juan Marichal,

Benito Santiago, Ivan DeJesus. I hear the announcer's voice crescendo upwards, climax in a flurry of play calling, then diminuendo. Chico Carrasquel. I bet these guys got to play baseball all day. Like Mickey Mantle. Mantle played baseball from dawn to dusk whenever the Oklahoma winter and winds subsided. He and his buddies rotated at lunch as one boy peeled off to eat and then returned, letting another boy go. Now, mothers feel their sons are only safe at, well, home. Or at hockey practice, where the mothers sit and observe until the young lad is big enough to attend on his own. With plenty of other responsible adults around to keep an eye on the coach. Baseball requires a lot of repetition until the basic skills are automatic. No wonder there are more and more players from other countries.

Some names summon up nineteenth century America: Ty Cobb, Cy Young. Others are so evocative of who we are: Joe DiMaggio, Jim Konstanty, Carl Yastrzemski, Harmon Killebrew. You couldn't make up names like these. I do not know one man named Orel or Minnie or Satchel. They are a phonetic phonebook of America.

Maybe baseball is a more cerebral game than you might guess at first glance. Maybe it's really intellectual, like chess. When looking at a particular bunting possibility, you have to be able to recall 900 other possibilities. "Ah, ha! My foolish opponent has opened with his Nimzovitch-Larsen attack (the *Dutch* variation)!"

I hope baseball is really smart because I grew up in Chicago. Winters were tough, but so was spring. Spring meant excited, anticipatory Cubs fans crowding the Addison Street el stop and mobbing Wrigley field, Cubbie pennants clutched in their hands. Why? Why were they so happy? They just made me crazy. Year after year. My own sister loved the Cubs. Everyone knew they would slink home with baleful, hurt faces. If you asked them why they were such fans, they would go on and on about the park, the ivy on the walls. I decided the sports teams in Chicago were so bad because the politics were so good. I mean, the elections were a hoot and a holler.

Since I failed to attach to the Cubs (and the White Sox were on the South Side), what happened to my baseball libido? While I was in grammar school at the Lincoln School, there were four Subway Series in New York. The Yankees won three of them. Once, probably in 1955 when the Underdogs won, a TV set appeared in the hall at the base of the statue of the great man himself (Lincoln, not Johnny Podres). This upending of priorities by the adults was alarming and delightful to me. I admired the Yankees. All good Americans root for the underdog. But let's be honest. We don't mind success, money, skill or cold, reptilian confidence either. I'm sorry. I enjoy watching Derek Jeter. (Fortunately my sons do not take me seriously so my moral ignorance regarding the Yankees has not damaged their enthusiasm for the Twins.) To really *love* baseball you have to be a statistics nut. The meaning of every play lies in the history of every player, each trade, each owner, each bunt. Who needs it? Idiot savants. Now football, walk in, look at the field, check the score and time, and you've got it. It's territorial. It goes way back to when nation fought nation in declared wars. It moves. It precedes the UN, which was designed to stop such territorial marches. And basketball—why not just watch the last five minutes?

George Will, a student—make that scholar—of the game, made the following observation: "Baseball is a game of episodic action. Discrete events stand out. The players are dispersed around a large space. And it is the American sport with the longest season and longest history."[1] Will also remarks:

> Other sports are played in a strictly defined space, like a basketball court or football field. However baseball has what one writer (George Grella) calls 'potential for infinity.' Even foul balls are in play until they land in the stands, and if you removed the stands, the field of play would extend forever through 360 degrees. The republic, the planet, the universe would be an extended baseball field. What a jolly idea.[2]

An eternity that is baseball? Still, I am concerned about the lack of pick-up ball in my town. I'm concerned because I am an American. Like many Americans I grieve over the decay of our society, the vulgarity of our culture, the sewer that is TV. Sports do not create character in a person, but sports do bring out and develop traits inherent in the person. Important lessons are learned on the pitcher's mound; steps are taken into manhood.

Our national pastime became much more serious when the events of 9/11 pushed the World Series into

November, because it had to be held in New York. Bravado, bravery and a battered flag opened the game at Yankee Stadium. The president pitched the first ball with F-16's circling the air space above a packed stadium. We had to know we could still "Play ball!" When things get really hard, the nation needs a pastime. This is when baseball becomes pure relief, a great way to get back to ourselves.

Current baseball players are bigger and they're better. But where are the sandlot games? Is anyone keeping an eye on baseball the way economists keep an eye on leading economic indicators? Is our culture just too down and dumb for the brain strain it takes to enjoy the game? What if baseball finally is so organized, so hard to tell from practicing the piano, that it dies? Can we trust this to Generation X…the Millenials? What happened to dinner?

Probably the death of baseball would be a good thing. It might trigger a renewal of our society. A kid somewhere would pick up a rock and hit it with a stick. Another kid would go get the rock. Another kid would see this and wander over. It is surely something deep in Americans that will always be there.

Somewhere there is laughter and somewhere children shout, but not in my town. It is the bottom of the eighth and the Southwest Self Esteems are being crunched by the Edina Egoists. Those parents are relaxed and happy, chatting and musing about trying out for the traveling league next year. The Southwest parents are hanging in there, but longing for it to be over. After all, it's 9:00 and they haven't eaten yet. The kids are learning to endure but would have switched players around long ago to make it more fun, if it had been up to them.

When Ted Turner lost the World Series to Canada, I had an ominous foreboding that something was wrong in this favored land. But I am a pessimist. Waveland Avenue is still filled with kids who couldn't get into Wrigley Field and are hoping for a ball to come flying into the street. They give new meaning to the word "hope." Surely baseball is bigger than baby boomers and the torch is being passed to a new generation. Anyway, I saw it on TV. Our flag is still there.

I Feel Pretty

There is a moment, I like to think, in every girl's life when she senses she has an emerging womanhood that will give her power over men. She has looked in the mirror and noticed a womanly curve where there was flatness. Or she has pulled her hair up in front of a mirror and observed her profile for the first time. Ambivalence, even fear may combine with a realization that in this light, and at this angle, yes, she has allure. If there is a boy she likes, or a picture of some current troubadour fastened to her wall, it may create a certain giddiness. She may even go a little nuts.

In Tolstoy's *War and Peace*, a book about courtship (followed by the darker novel *Anna Karenina*, which is about marriage), Natasha has such a moment. She is sixteen and knows that at least two men have fallen in love with her:

> It's amazing how clever I am, and how...Ah, how charming she is,' she went on, speaking to herself in the third person and imagining it was some very intelligent, the most intelligent and best of men who was saying this about her. 'She has everything, everything,' continued this man, 'she is extraordinarily intelligent, charming... and then she is pretty, remarkably pretty, and graceful—she swims and rides splendidly, and what a voice! One can really say a marvelous voice!'[1]

This is a private moment of indulgence in vanity and happiness. Natasha is in love with herself. At this moment the girl stops hoping and knows that happiness is very, very possible. In fact, it will happen to her. She has what it takes to win Leonardo DiCaprio. It's the moment when a chaste and sheltered girl is ready to come to terms with her destiny, to love and be loved.

Maria, in *West Side Story*, is about to embark on a quixotic romance that is as passionate as any mid-life crisis. And as crazy. Picture Natalie Wood in the movie as she sees herself in the mirror trying on various poses, attitudes and articles of finery with giddy abandon. "See the pretty girl in that mirror there!"[2] Her handmaidens laugh and tease her. The sadder but wiser Rita Moreno (Anita) is scornful and concerned, because she knows the ending of *Romeo and Juliet*. (Anita, we suspect, was not so protected or allowed much of a courtship before the reality of erotic experience.) But who can resist a maiden who has been protected and shown self-control as well, letting fly with this egotistical debut?

Well, this is the way the well-brought-up young ladies behave in literature. In real life the more aggressive girls have the guile and passive allure of the Terminator. The year my younger son turned fifteen he was one of the youngest boys in his class. The girls, turning sixteen, decided he was the closest they were going to get to Tom Cruise. They began a campaign that made Napoleon look like a slacker. While I would be resting on Sunday, they were planning Monday's party and Wednesday's drama du jour. They would call him on conference calls. One called from a thousand miles away. I threw my body in front of four or five of them.

My son, who had received years of instruction from me about the wiles of women, decided I "just didn't get it." A lamb to slaughter. He laughed, flirted and generally enjoyed their attention. I thought someone had opened up his head and vacuumed out his brains, but I also developed my mouth muscles. The game was heightened because the girls all knew I was part of it. If they got him they would be defeating me too. What fun.

Women usually know what other women are up to. They sense it. They warn their husbands about females in the office, and their husbands, if they are wise, heed their advice. That young men can be easily seduced is common knowledge. It could be engraved on public buildings.

For at the window of my house
I looked through my lattice,
And saw among the simple,
I perceived among the youths,
A young man devoid of understanding,
Passing along the street near her corner;
And he took the path to her house
In the twilight, in the evening,
In the black and dark night.
And there a woman met him...—PROVERBS 7:6-10

This is a kind of predatory, adult seduction. Natasha and Maria are experiencing a normal, giddy moment of adolescence. But what I do not understand is how do *men* know and write so well about this terribly private moment in an adolescent girl's life?

In the *Mikado*—well, if you don't know the plot I'm not going to try to explain it to you here—William S. Gilbert wrote a gorgeous paean to this moment. When Yum-Yum has won the love of Nanki-Poo and has been lovingly dressed by her handmaidens for the wedding, she sings a song of such eloquent narcissism that I wonder if anyone actually stops to think of what she is saying. (I once read that at some place on the globe, the *Mikado* is being performed every day of the year.)

The sun, whose rays
Are all ablaze
   With ever-living glory,
Does not deny
His majesty—

He scorns to tell a story!
He don't exclaim,
 'I blush for shame,
 So kindly be indulgent'...
I mean to rule the earth,
 As he the sky—
We really know our worth,
 The sun and I!

My goodness! What was Yum-Yum thinking about in the ladies' seminary? (Relational fantasies are pornography for women.)

Not enough that Yum-Yum likens herself to the sun, she is also the moon:

Observe his flame,
That placid dame,
 The moon's Celestial Highness;
There's not a trace
Upon her face
 Of diffidence or shyness:
She borrows light
That, through the night,
 Mankind may all acclaim her!
And, truth to tell,
She lights up well,
 So I, for one, don't blame her!
Ah, pray make no mistake,
 We are not shy;
We're very wide-awake,
 The moon and I!

We are enchanted with this wonderful braggart. It's a ravishing moment in the operetta. Now, imagine a man singing such a song. It would be a joke like the 1920's novelty song "I Love Me." But young girls can even get away with a *duet* devoted to themselves! No one smirks at the scene in the movie *Meet Me in St. Louis* when Judy Garland, who plays Esther, and her sister Rose are primping at their dressing table for a party designed to snag the new boy next door. Judy Garland is confiding to Rose that she intends to let John Truett kiss her. Suddenly they see themselves in the vanity mirror:

Rose: It would have been nice if I could have been a brunette.
Esther: Yes, you should have been a brunette. Then nothing could have stopped us. Just think how we would have looked going out together. You with your raven black hair and me with my auburn.

Later at Christmastime, getting ready for the "the smartest ball of the season," Rose is initiating her sister into womanhood, the pain of the corset. The two are plotting how they are going to snare their respective love interests and foil their competition. Judy Garland has never worn a corset before and can hardly breathe or sit down:

Rose: It'll be worth it. If we can create a breathtaking effect it will be simple to monopolize all the worthwhile men.

Esther: Exactly. There's only going to be about twenty men. I should hope. You can handle ten?
Rose: Well, seven or eight.
Esther: If you can guarantee eight, I can handle the rest of them.[3]

To love and be loved means to sacrifice endlessly, to change and become a drink offering poured out to one's children. One gets married and has children to enhance one's life and add to one's own happiness and standing in society. "Marriage is harder than I imagined," the bride thinks. There is a lot of adjusting to be made. But children will come and adore her unconditionally. They will round out her decorating. They brighten up Christmas. Their clothing is adorable. She will be so good at it. She will not make the mistakes her own mother made.

What a surprise to find out that the task of motherhood will not enhance her own self but will eliminate self. Her svelte figure is shot. With this demanding new baby she can't even take a shower before noon! She is exhausted! She's too busy and tired to have long discussions with her husband about his job. They need to make dates and discipline themselves to not talk about the kids. Then, financial ruin. "How are we going to put five kids through college?"

Finally, according to the Plan, the children leave. What kind of a plan is that? What is left? A job? Grandchildren? Friends fade away if they were really cohorts of those heroic child rearing years. Hopefully, there is still a spouse around. Remember how this story started? Better spruce up that friendship and develop an interest in putting on showers for other young narcissists.

Why is a moment of self adoration so charming in literature, theater and song? Because it is real. Because we recognize ourselves. We were young once. It is charming to see a pretty girl flushed with excitement. And it is only possible if innocence has been protected into late adolescence. For years the girl has wondered if anyone could love her. Could it happen to her? Will she ever meet Mr. Bingley?

The girl's self-love shows a huge capacity for love, and it occurs on the cusp of maturity. The gleeful child is hugging herself; the girl in the mirror is a woman. Let her have her fun.

Everybody Must Get Stoned

My loathing for the lawn increases. The weeds are outgrowing the lawn, always an iffy project under eight oaks with one dog and owners who were raised in cities. The lawn needs more attention than a newborn infant. But that is nothing compared to my feelings about the English Cottage Garden. My backyard is a graveyard for hundreds of flowers, most guaranteed to grow here in the permafrost.

I am numb. Never again will a rosebush break my heart. Never again will I fall for the gorgeous pictures in gardening porn books. After planting hundreds of periwinkle plants I was rewarded with a breathtaking blanket of blue flowers under an old, flowering crab that was a cloud of pink blossoms. Well, the crab succumbed to a fungus and the periwinkle receded to small patches.

I paid for that bit of Zone hubris. Lying liars will tell you that Minneapolis is Zone 4, but it is really Zone 3.

My last victims: three astilbe. They died from a cascade of problems, beginning with neglect. Left in the pots too long, they got dry, then a nice nitrogen burn from drenching them with a watering can that had Miracle Gro in it, then no mulch, etc., etc. The usual squalid tale.

Ours was once a woodsy—surprisingly woodsy— peaceful and private dead end in a large suburb. We shared the block with mostly elderly people who happily suffered our kids' bikes and rope swings on their driveways and ravines. They gave the funnest parties in the world. They waved and grew frail and finally blew away into a better world.

Their houses were sold to younger families whose children livened up the place. But they had vision and their own backyard dreams. For two summers here we heard nothing but trees being chopped down and chippers running. Once I put on earphones and a video to escape from the din of deforestation. I sat on the coffee table which vibrated beneath me. I could even feel it in the basement.

The road rattled as ravines were filled in and sod rolled out. Our woods was being gentrified. Dump trucks would run every six minutes down our street. But once the dust settled, what emerged were beautiful gardens, zone hardy with color in every season, magazine perfect.

To do this an amazing number of boulders was bought. The backyards on the bluff side are terraced with boulders which support hundreds of loads of landfill. Flatbed trucks arrived regularly, rattling down the street to deliver enormous loads of boulders. Even neighbors only marginally interested in this would buy a boulder and plunk it down on the corner of their lot.

Covering a bald spot?

Why do they do this? There is something compelling about defining a border. The American family is no longer a strong or stable institution; maybe they are trying to batten down a corner of the lawn, anyway. Add some security. But if you drive around on other streets in Bloomington the effect of using boulders as lawn decoration is…words fail. Maybe a persuasive traveling salesman representing Monolith Inc. visited here in the sixties. The best answer I've heard is that "everyone does it." A friend says that in her neighborhood, which is filled with people my age, "a certain age," neighbors are having their boulders removed—a youthful indiscretion they no longer want to decorate with plantings.

A rogue Stonehenge gene?

And there's the rub: "youthful." Being a solid twenty years older than my young neighbors, I am fading out of the energy zone. AARP is looking better to me. I am part of the Old Guard. I couldn't keep up if I tried. While the cottage garden was purportedly carried on in England as a desultory, puttering hobby, I've read enough to know that there were several gardening maniacs in old England who turned it into a high energy retirement or dipped substantially into the Rothschild fortune to move earth and transport azaleas from Tibet. It didn't take me long to realize I am an armchair gardener.

My husband and I made a heroic effort to fit into suburban life. We both spent our early years in suburbs but don't seem to remember much about it. Being late-life parents, we really did not know how to live in the suburbs when we bought our house. Like people entering a foreign culture, we learned the hard way about a lot of things. The furnace guy explained that what had taken out the furnace was getting the ducts cleaned. And so forth. We went to Red Lobster for the first time when I was in my forties. We are the worst grass farmers in the world. (I think that what is killing our lawn is grass seed.) But like a lot of people we are prisoners of our children, who are teenagers and change of address is very damaging to their fragile systems.

But what ho? How now? Lying on my desk is a gift certificate for Wayside Gardens which my sister, Zone 5, sent me at Christmas. It couldn't hurt to look. Hostas are safe. Of course I end up spending twice the amount the gift certificate was worth. My husband and I dig out bushels of weeds, go through two bottles of Round Up. I sketch out a new garden. We finally get it in, water and wait expectantly. Is new life stirring in our veins? Fresh sap running through our jaded systems?

Perhaps we are just growing up. In his book *In the Shadow of Memory*, Floyd Skloot quotes Viktor Frankl: "Man must, Frankl believes, 'temper his efforts to the chances that are offered.'" Of course, Skloot is describing his heroic journey of living with brain injury, not wishful gardening.

I never really learned the streets in downtown St. Paul because I knew we would only live here two or three years. After twenty-one years, it's time to accept that Minnesota is in fact my home; we live here. This is my lot and we will continue to tidy up the forest floor. Accepting the horticultural possibilities is a trivial challenge, quite doable.

One day, we too will wave our hands, move on and

hand our oaks and lawn over to a gardening enthusi-ast. I wish them well. And we will go back to what we know how to do—pushing an elevator button.

Homeschooling for Dummies

I describe myself as a recovering stay-at-home mom. I stayed out of the work force, happily, for about seventeen years and raised two sons. I even homeschooled for six years. I was part of a dynamic, powerful group of exhausted women who tried to and did support each other. We also kept an eye on each other to make sure our little darlings were getting every possible advantage that other kids were. And they got them.

Some of us were refugees from schools that were incompetent. Some of us were rescuing kids who weren't thriving, kids who were going down the tubes. Some of us felt called to be the person who nurtured our children's hearts, minds and souls. Lots of us were control freaks or just didn't know who they were without their children.

I personally was dragged kicking and screaming into homeschooling because the private school my sons attended was clearly having problems. A friend of mine raved about homeschooling as we sat together during Little League games. I thought it was a little sick to keep kids out of school, but like many of my friends I had heard terrible stories about how toxic and brutal public schools can be, especially junior high. I continued to rebel until late August, when I finally ordered some books. A friend called and suggested one supplier. Then another. I discovered that there is a consumer paradise of suppliers with glossy catalogs.

Having finally decided to homeschool, I thought, "Okay. Well then, in case we ever come out of the Dark Ages and anyone ever wants to know about Western Civilization, they can ask my kids." A quotation that inspired me then was: "There have always been civilized people and they have always been surrounded by barbarians." I spent hundreds of dollars on splendid books I never knew existed. I was in love.

I wasn't alone. I learned there is a highly networked underground of homeschoolers who are generous with their information. That same year *Time* magazine ran an article on homeschooling. It featured a black woman living in the Beltway area who had taken her kids out of school. She said that whatever she accomplished at home "couldn't be worse." The picture showed three bright-looking children seated at a kitchen counter studying. And to do this, the mother had taught herself to read. That was the year Hillary Clinton was voted Mother of the Year.

My boys had guessed what was up and told me there was no way they would be homeschooled. My husband and I sat them down, explained that this indeed was going to happen. I showed them my diplomas and we described the trip they would take to Disneyland with all the money we saved after taking them out of private school. We also threw in hockey. They looked doubtful, but we had made a firm decision, a strong presentation, and they were only six and eight. Still, they looked dubious until I wrote the vowels on the dry erase board: "a,e,i,o,u and sometimes y." Their eyes widened with respect.

I learned that homeschoolers will organize and scream loudly to protect their hard-won rights to be "self-educating." The movement was pioneered by a variety of people, some for religious and some for non-sectarian reasons. They shared the view that parents have the right to determine their children's education, as long as state requirements are satisfied. In 2008 it was estimated that 2.0 to 2.5 million children in grades K to 12 are home educated nationally. While the percentage remains low (under 5%), it appears the population continues to grow.[1]

Secular and Christian organizations serve this counter culture with information, legal defense and well-attended conventions. Support groups and co-operatives abound. I paid reasonable dues to a watch-dog group, the Home School Legal Defense Association (HSLDA). I (who have never joined any club in my life) joined one association, at least two support groups and a kind of collective school.

The first year I flailed about, shocked to discover that my older boy, who was by then in third grade, knew no math facts and had trouble reading. Why had he scored in the 90's on standardized tests? His brother, who had taught himself to read in kindergarten, rolled around on the floor in boredom. It was a real soup. Finally I hired a mentor who told me that the first year was "a year of inventory taking." I heartily agreed. I hadn't realized what a short-tempered jerk I was. If you want to realize what a miserable person you are, just become a parent. The new mother may notice that her six-month-old has picked up one of her bad habits. So young? Or, she may confess with dismay, "I lied to Jason today." I had been shocked to find myself stealing my toddlers' Halloween candy, after putting it out of their reach. Lying and stealing will lead to threats, bribery, extortion, blackmail: "If you don't stop that, I'm going to call Daddy!" Homeschooling returns a sense of heroism.

I discovered my kids loved to learn, and teaching them was something I was born to do. We also learned to love each other a lot, and our energies and hearts were turned to home just as the outside world was beginning to pull them away. This pull can worry a parent; the parent can get a little paranoid. Many very conservative mothers are part of the second wave of Boomer parents and they remember all too well what they were or weren't wearing at Woodstock. How easy it was to crumble the social consensus that existed at that time in the U.S. They will put a lot of energy into giving their children some innocence, scouring thrift shops to find something modest for their daughters to wear.

There is a stream of "Lost Innocence" that flows through American culture, a collective childhood that is remembered as free and safe. In homeschooling there seemed to be two paradigms for virtue that were displayed in all the catalogs and to some degree fired the imaginations of parents. One was pioneer America, *Little House on the Prairie*. And the other was a Neo-Victorian ideal of domestic girlhood with blue velvet dresses and pianos. The hope is that these "uberkinder" will put Humpty Dumpty together again.

No two mothers school the same way and that is the joy of it. A lot of time in elementary school is taken up with workbooks, standing in line to go to lunch, waiting with your arm propped up in the air with your other arm until the teacher can answer your question. One of the first things I did was toss out the vocabulary workbooks. I decided my boys would learn English through immersion. I would talk to them. They would read books. We sat down to dinner as a family (no small effort) and conversed. I usually set the table with linen, cloth napkins and candles and we talked to Dad about everything.

The days were ours. We slept late, did math first and then the boys chose their subjects. Usually they practiced their instruments after lunch. Our TV had kind of died so we used it as a video monitor for eight years. And since homeschooling is so efficient, recess often consisted of two hours building snow forts or sledding.

Homeschooling moms teach all day while maintaining their homes and God forbid, the cottage industry the catalogs tell them they can do since they are home all day anyway. At night they go to their co-op meetings, desperately hoping to get a glimpse of how to teach composition, get some clue about their son with ADHD and dyslexia. Maybe they just burst into tears about how overwhelmed they are and can't their husband see that having six kids and no dishwasher is very hard? I looked around at one such meeting and wondered if such a spirit of resistance to the state would not have delighted Thomas Jefferson.

There is, however, a dark side to homeschooling. The chapter entitled, *The Day Mom Called Her Child Stupid*, or the repeated scene where Daddy opens the door to see Mom in tears surrounded by kids, some of whom are also crying. These days are not unique to homeschooling, just not printable, and you certainly won't find them in the catalogs containing at least two family pictures of mothers of thirteen children, one of whom has just gotten her masters degree at home! I actually met one of those children at a homeschooling support group and she said, "Well, if you look closely at those pictures, one of the children is usually crying."

Most of the elementary schools in my town, Bloomington, were built between 1950 and 1963. I've only been in them to vote and take my sons to community basketball programs. To relieve the boredom, I would explore the school. The halls usually sported a collection of artwork, snowmen all crafted with the same materials and looking very much alike. The sensible, if slightly socialist, reason for this is that young children don't usually have artistic ability and so if all their artwork looks alike, no one feels bad. The walls were usually concrete blocks, glazed a beige or lemony color. The girls' bathrooms had steel stalls once enameled pink but now quite worn. The floor was square brown tiles; the hallways were linoleum. Posters on the walls exhorted students with some popular bromide: "Tommy Tolerance Says!"

At home, we worked in an upstairs bedroom with one large window that looked out on the upper branches of a large oak. The walls had originally been wallpapered in a print very popular in the '80's, small blue diamonds on a white background. I added a large border that showed an old-fashioned, painterly scene of a boy and his dog watching sailboats on a river. We cleaned and painted old school desks and put laminated alphabets on the corners of them. As the years went by, we added homemade timelines which included things important to us, such as when the bicycle was invented and the pictures of classical composers. There was a happy clutter of books; a crystal hung on the window and cast prismatic colors on the hall. Pets would stray in and "make the children laugh and play."

It was the best thing our family has ever done. I had a career that was demanding and fascinating. But I had no vision for it after sixth grade. I looked at the back of the algebra book; all those brackets and sigmas made my head swim. "Gallia est omnis divisa in partes tres." No. There was no going back to all that. But I could do grammar school and fortunately found a school nearby to finish the job.

There may be a post-homeschooling syndrome. My friends, looking back on those years, sigh and say how happy they were, but somehow reinvented themselves. We were so busy, so important. My husband, whose job in advertising set records for crazy, envied me because, as he put it, "What you're doing matters."

Do the children have trouble separating? Both of my boys entered "real school" in seventh grade. The first day for my older boy was okay for me, but on the second day I was alone. I started crying and couldn't stop. I called my husband at work and could only gasp out glottal answers to the questions he asked: "Was there an accident? Is everyone all right? Is anyone in the hospital? Is this what I think it is?" For the first and only time he drove home to have lunch with me. I was still crying. I sobbed while making him a ham and cheese sandwich. He said, "Well, do you want to get out the baby videos and just wallow in it?" I nodded. We did and they were funny and pretty soon my crying subsided and we were laughing.

I expected something pretty much the same when his brother left. He was younger and had been at home since kindergarten. But it was time to go. He was talking to the dog. He was also quite anxious and his brother patiently answered all his questions. Since this boy had been homeschooled for six years, he didn't know how to ask to go to the bathroom, get from one room to another, get his milk at lunch. I watched as he left. Their dad's convertible backed out the driveway and he leaned out. With a mixture of real excitement and bravado he yelled, "You're going to cry mom. And I did not brush my teeth!"

The garage door shut and I was really alone for the

first time in sixteen years. I was also fired. I was skewered. I spent the first day in a frenzy of cleaning till I was lame from running up and down the stairs. Finally, order. Then the depression sank in. I had no interest in all the projects I thought I would finally have time to do when the kids were gone. I hated the house; it was the kids I loved. The nest was too empty, too soon. For the first time in eighteen years I felt like having a drink—at noon. I became a manic volunteer then slowly adjusted.

I often drove by places so nostalgic of the years when my sons were little that I had to go in and relive the dear, old joys. Or I had to drive by. The library was tough. I love books and my sons loved to climb the Scotch pines on the lawn outside. They would do this as long as I would stand to watch them. Afterwards the three of us would go get doughnuts. The other day I went to the library, which had been closed for remodeling. Someone, probably at a lawyer's suggestion, had lopped off all the low hanging limbs on the Scotch pines. The interior was wired for the internet and suddenly very crowded. It was all so hard. I had to summon up all the courage I developed in Kindergarten to go it alone.

Was it worth it? I know lots of kids who went to the public schools here. Every week the community paper arrives on my doorstep and I read about the "Student Achievers of the Week." They look like compassionate, good-looking, athletic, vibrant young adults whose "Mentor Connection project in micro-electrical mechanical systems at the University of Minnesota will be presented at an international conference this fall." They surely survived the dreary environment, as talent always will. They look like they outclass my coddled children any day.

So, was I led to homeschool? One son was gifted, easily bored—a class clown in a class of two. The other boy was dyslexic with the unusual gifts in math and physics that often accompany dyslexia. Both became good students with creative, probing minds. In Tolstoy's *Anna Karenina*, Anna is separated from her young son Seryozha, who is being educated by an unsympathetic tutor and a cold, distant father:

> He was nine years old, he was a child, but he knew his own mind, it was dear to him, and he guarded it as the eyelid guards the eye, and without the key of love he let no one into it. His instructors complained that he did not want to learn, but his mind was full to the brim with a thirst for knowledge.[2]

Homeschooling is the road less traveled for good reasons. It is very, very hard. But it is not as hard as watching your child fail. This is why mothers with no experience, no training and no time will try it. They know their own children better than anyone else possibly could and they believe they can accomplish, one on one, what cannot be done in a classroom. Mothers know that they own the "key of love" and love needs no apologetic.

My first girlfriend, Jeannie.

Girlfriend

The soul selects her own society—
Then—shuts the Door—
To her divine majority—
—EMILY DICKINSON

Girlfriend is the reason I write. Girlfriend is the imaginary playmate I invented, I am guessing, around the age of three. When I was three my younger sister, the last of four daughters, was born and she undoubtedly yanked me off center stage. I imagine I hatched Girlfriend to salve my bruised ego, to entertain me. My mother once mentioned having to go back and open a bank door for Girlfriend, as she had not known that Girlfriend was accompanying us on that particular errand.

Around the age of five, when I entered Kindergarten,

I killed Girlfriend off. I explained that she had been heedlessly running around in the kitchen when she ran into a large knife that had been left jutting out of the table. It had sliced her in two. Later I must have gotten lonely. I briefly resurrected her and enjoyed some more golden playtimes before I finally explained that Girlfriend had been killed in a terrible car accident in Skokie, Illinois. (Skokie was a suburb just west of Evanston, Illinois, where I grew up.)

Evanston, Illinois – 1956

Such was the esteem with which I regarded Kindergarten that I knew no fully matriculated scholar would have a leftover from childhood like Girlfriend. My older sisters had gone to the Lincoln School and they had cashmere sweaters and Pendleton skirts. No. Miss Edna would never know about Girlfriend. But I am here to tell you that she is alive. She has been these fifty years or so. She is a great listener. She is very sympathetic. I talk to her all the time. She is a terrific editor. When I sit down to write a letter, it pours forth because I have already written it to Girlfriend in the car, where I live. By the time I get to typing, the dumbest stuff is gone. OKAY! YES! I talk to myself.

No. I mean, it looks like I'm talking to "myself." My younger son, Dan, delighted in discerning when I was talking to myself. (Like other children their age, my two boys were raised in the car. I saturated them with Mother Goose tapes and "Peter and the Wolf." I dislocated my shoulder dishing out sandwiches, Ritz Crackers and swats. I became expert at suddenly pulling over, putting the car in park and threatening that any boy who did not...but I digress.)

Dan knew I was talking to myself just by observing my eyebrows, or worse, hands. "Mom! You're talking to yourself!" "How'd you know?" I'd exclaim. At first it flustered and embarrassed me. Then I just went along with the game. Heck, now I just can't wait to be in a ward somewhere where I can babble on uninhibitedly.

That's not true. Unlike fiction writers, I have a fear of losing my mind. I was talking to a neighbor who said that she and her husband had recently had dinner with a couple who were both sixty-eight. "And, guess what?"

"What?" I asked.

"He's started a new business and she's written a novel."

"She did? How did she do that?"

"Well, she was writing down a family history for a reunion and she just started to fictionalize."

That to me is really scary. That's taking real people and changing them around as if they were little transformers. Anne Lamotte described something like that in *Bird by Bird*. She said that your character may be pursuing a man and then all of a sudden you realize you had her wrong, she is a homosexual. What? I just could never do that. Girlfriend is embarrassing enough. I never took any mind-altering drugs like LSD. I never wanted to see the sky turn into orange flames. I never wanted to burn out my brain with pot. I refused to learn Base 8 or whatever it was that wasn't decimal and had nothing to do with shopping. Tolstoy got so upset about the carnage of the War of 1812 he was describing in *War and Peace* that he threw trays full of dishes at his wife.

Once the thoughts emerge, however, they want to be shared. Michel de Montaigne began writing because his best friend died and so did their wonderful dinner conversations. It is true that Girlfriend is not Etienne de La Boétie. Still, she did die young. And she has the remarkable advantage of being there whenever I want to talk about me, me, me.

I have actually always had very nice friends who were girls, now women. None quite as simpatico as Girlfriend, but nonetheless, great friends. My grammar school friends were nice, innocent, athletic and intelligent. Pat just about killed me at kickball every day after school. Susie could play piano like nobody's business and we were so mutually devoted to Nancy Drew that we called each other up in fifth grade to finish reading the last paragraph of the last book simultaneously. Andy had great enthusiasm, great brains, and she sustained a two-year crush on the same boy.

High school consisted of two things: field hockey and

talking on the phone to Laurie and Abby. They got me through.

I picked a women's college. Having spent some time in the Alpha Chi Omega house where one of my sisters pledged, I knew by age eight I would never join a sorority. They had bunk beds, smelly nail polish, crinolines everywhere and paddles they spanked each other with. My college friends stuck close, even though I had moved back to Fort Apache (Chicago). Much visiting went on as they went to San Francisco to take sitar lessons with Ravi Shankar, during weddings, back and forths to New York, Cape Cod.

One of these friends, Quinton, lives in the Northwest where she forges exquisite poetry. She can fixate me for weeks with a single word. She is also the only person who knows who I was back in the day, in college, in Paris. Recently I sent her a blog and she just fell off her chair laughing. I hang on to her for dear life.

My sweet friend Sarah has lived in Bloomington for seven years—quite a change from Karachi. That I love her can only be known by anyone who knows how much I put off shopping, something we do together weekly. Sarah and I speak spirit to spirit. She has a great command of English and doubles over laughing at my jokes.

Marsha always calls if she has an extra symphony ticket. She prays for my children, our nation and everyone on earth. She has four wonderful sons. She is a gracious hostess who pulls pies out of the air. She is a great laugher. She has beaten breast cancer and invites ladies to her home every week where we pull down powers and principalities. She looks harmless, but Marsha is a force.

Marge is the neighbor to end all neighbors. She's sad if we don't use her swimming pool. Marge has taken countless photos of us and invites us over for holidays. Do you need a coffee urn for a reception? She was just going to get a new one and will deliver it to your door. Marge is also a great laugher.

Dede and I raised our children together. She has four boys and I have two. Years ago the boys would eagerly put together gingerbread houses decorated with candies and items we had seen on the covers of magazines that decorate the checkout counters of grocery stores. The boys were eager to do it because they knew they would be allowed, at the end of the evening, to smash the houses to smithereens. One year they all got air guns and the six boys and two husbands spent about an hour running about the basement, kitchen and backyard shooting each other and having realistic, very loud fun. They wound down by setting off fireworks. Dede and I huddled in a corner of the living room sipping Christmas tea. Fortunately, she is a great laugher.

My neighbor Lila is a family artist. She is always thinking of new ways to celebrate her children and grandchildren and is instinctively nurturing. I am not a confident hostess and Lila always tells me, "It will be fine." It is. She is like Queen Elizabeth. Everyone behaves around her. She shapes you up in her bemused way. She never screws up and yet everyone loves her. She laughs heartily and welcomes the coming years.

Blue left her career (which included a write-up in

Time) to be a full-time mother and even homeschooled her daughter. Of course, she ran a co-op for home-schoolers, and if you couldn't make a meeting, she doused you with love, never guilt. She has poured her considerable administrative skills into her family, political causes, her Bible studies and her duties on the boards of a college and a large church. Blue sends lots of joke emails and has a great giggle.

I have been friends with Betsy for more years than either of us would like to mention. Talk about your different drummer. We did the "dress for success" thing together in the marketing department of Continental Bank in Chicago in the '70's. She went upwards in bank marketing and then, one day, moved to California and opened a gift shop. Her store is like her: full of fun, whimsy and work. Once her house was in disrepair and I suggested it would be cheaper if she just got twenty cats—her neighbors would just write her off. She said she'd been written off long ago, and I sensed the joy, the smartness of what I had been fighting: maturity.

Betsy is a great laugher. Sorry, she's my friend, not yours. You cannot go to her house, eat fresh lobster, sit on her patio in the Mediterranean climate and drink bottles of Dos Equis she has squeezed limes into, after mussels in cream sauce at the local eatery, three minutes from her house. Sorry.

It may seem like I have a lot of friends, but actually it is Diana who does. I call her the Mayor of Dianaville. Since I know her, I don't have to go to the trouble of knowing, well, *everyone*. She has a quality that tells you your worries, your secret anguish are safe with her. She has a quiet spirit. She loves music and her family, her three sons (seeing a pattern here?), and has been a valiant prayer warrior for them and everyone else. She loves to laugh and loves you if you make her laugh.

I have only told you about a few of my friends. The others would be too embarrassed to see their names in print but are as lovely, gracious and generous as the ones mentioned here. Do any of these ladies know about Girlfriend? If they do, they are too merciful to let on. I picture my friends as a bouquet of flowers, each quite different, beautiful in her own way, leaning over me in my coffin, saying, "Didn't they do a nice job with her?" Really, they should say "them."

Doubt Truth to Be a Liar

It beseems us better friends to avenge than fruitlessly
mourn them.
—BEOWULF (ll.1384-85)

In the dungeon where I do the laundry I go through the
pockets of my son's pants. This didn't used to be a bad
job: firecrackers, candy wrappers, the occasional dead
frog. But now he is in high school and I find a note from
a girl. It is not okay. He knows I will read it. She knows
I will read it. Did *he* read this? I think I am supposed to
call her mother and create a big drama. How did I get
enmeshed in this game of Spy vs. Spy, Parent vs.
Teenager? I decide the note is a pack of lies, throw it out
and pray. My son, a pretty happy guy, finally gets tired
of being yanked around and ends this relationship. I

learn the meaning of phrases like "worried to death."

It has given me sympathy for Polonius. You remember Polonius. He is the court advisor in *Hamlet,* the father of Ophelia. Polonius is a sententious, "prating fool." Polonius is a loser parent, a windbag. Still, he is worried. A widower, he suspects Ophelia has become young Hamlet's lover—so does her brother. For a loving father, this is heartbreaking; but for a professional courtier, such a match would definitely be a brilliant step up in the world. Polonius manipulates the kids until he gets Ophelia to give him Hamlet's love letters to her, which he immediately shows to the king and queen, Gertrude and Claudius. I just want out of this murky, dank basement.

It's not all that great upstairs. Our older boy is a senior in high school and has let several deadlines for college applications pass by. He applied to one university and then let other deadlines go by. His father and I nagged, reminded him of very nice things like how much money we had spent taking him to Colorado, and eventually just wrung our hands. In mid-January, I watched him sit and stare at a half-finished essay and then go out for a walk. He was paralyzed by indecision and confusion, a veritable Hamlet. And I peeked through the blinds looking for the red glow of a cigarette in the dark night.

Polonius is also worried about college life. Laertes, Ophelia's older brother, is on his way to finish his studies in Paris. After lecturing him "to thine own self be true" during the big college send off, Polonius hires an agent to spy on his son. He tells him to infiltrate Parisian circles who would know the young Danes there, to spread and get some gossip on Laertes. Blithering this nefarious scheme to Renaldo, Polonius soon warms to his subject, routine stuff for a Renaissance court:

POLONIUS
> Take you as 'twere some distant knowledge of him,
> As thus, 'I know his father and his friends, And in
> part him'—do you mark this, Reynaldo?

REYNALDO
> Ay, very well, my lord.

POLONIUS
> 'And in part him, but,' you may say, 'not well,
> But if't be he I mean, he's very wild,
> Addicted so and so.' And there put on him
> What forgeries you please; marry, none so rank
> As may dishonor him—take heed of that—
> But, sir, such wanton, wild, and usual slips
> As are companions noted and most known
> To youth and liberty.

RENALDO
> As gaming, my lord.

POLONIUS
> Ay, or drinking, fencing, swearing, quarreling,
> Drabbing (whoring) You may go so far. (II.1.13- 26)

No one is sorry when Polonius is killed with a dagger thrust, hiding behind an arras to spy on Hamlet. No one except poor Ophelia who finally cracks. Sort of.

Hamlet is a gold mine of family dysfunction, written when Shakespeare had years enough to reflect on his own shotgun wedding and to experience his daughters' adolescence. (His son, Hamnet, had died at age eleven.) How the adults in this play spy on their children and how the children play-act to fool the adults. They are all consummate liars. Hamlet pretends to be mad, Ophelia feigns innocence and compliance, Gertrude pretends she cannot understand what's troubling her son and hires more college kids to spy on Hamlet. Plays within plays within plays.

I missed a lot of this at age eighteen when I took an entire semester of Shakespeare. Now that I am much older and have a better edition, not to mention teenagers, I wonder that Shakespeare is wasted on the young. Or that they are even allowed to read it. Never mind the gender bending, I recently sat down to enjoy *The Tempest* and was so repulsed by a vulgar reference that I did not get past Act I, Scene 1. (He's waiting. He knows I'll come back. I always do.)

Shakespeare was in his mid-thirties when he wrote *Hamlet.* The young people are infinitely more complex than those in *Romeo and Juliet,* written about five years earlier. In both plays the children are doomed by the sins of the parents. The feuding Capulets and Montagues have created civil strife that fuels the local gang violence. The plot is driven by erotic energy. The adult strictures and foibles that doom the two youngsters are highly artificial and seem as senseless as the suicides that end the play. The parents in *Romeo and Juliet* are concerned, but distant and easy to fool. Juliet's nurse is a foolish co-conspirator, abetting Juliet in her impolitic marriage as she might get her a forbidden sweet. The audience, of course, is on the side of young love. Who can't sympathize with such an idealistic first love, hormonal spillage and parents who "just don't get it"? It is a cocktail of teen behaviors, of "leap before you look" and rambunctious infatuation. Hamlet and Ophelia are darker, unnervingly close to home with complex relationships to their parents.

While Romeo is allowed to just be an adolescent, Hamlet never seems young. His bawdy thrusts at Ophelia are jaded, unnatural. He is easily played by older actors, but an aging Romeo is often comic.

In *Hamlet* the erotic energy is spent in a waste of shame. When the play opens, both young and old are trapped in the dark consequences of a murderous mid-life crisis and the young people cannot get on with their lives; they are checkmated by the king and queen. The young men won't finish college and Hamlet won't marry the girl next door—he has to murder his uncle. Hamlet, who had been in college in Germany, had returned home for his father's funeral and his mother's "o'erhasty marriage." His father was murdered by Hamlet's uncle while taking his daily nap. Asleep in the orchard with his beard streaked with silver, Hamlet's father is the picture of senescence. One can easily imagine that Gertrude was bored and her unmarried brother-in-law, the younger one, became an exciting diversion. Bedding and bed-hopping was a luxury that the rich could indulge in during the work day and kept the courts interesting. This "incestuous" marriage would move many in Shakespeare's audience closer to the edge of their seats, because they could remember all too well the horrific consequences of Henry VIII's doubt over the sanctity of his marriage to his sister-in-law.

Shakespeare is in his element here portraying pain and betrayal. A happy marriage was the formulaic end to comedies. While eye conceits abound in his work, one senses he never experienced a "Good Morrow to our Waking Souls." His virtuous women are either Petrarchan ideals as in "Who is Sylvia?" or types of Elizabeth I such as Portia, who rules with her commanding wit, wisdom and felicity of speech.

Ophelia is tragically alone. She has no mother, no nurse, no chaperone. Happy and confident at the beginning of the play, she takes her brother's overlong lecture (the apple does not fall far from the tree) about being used by Hamlet in stride with witty repartee:

> I shall the effect of this good lesson keep
> As watchman to my heart, but good my brother,
> Do not as some ungracious pastors do,
> Show me the steep and thorny way to heaven,
> Whiles like a puffed and reckless libertine
> Himself the primrose path of dalliance treads
> And recks not his own rede. (I.3.44-50)

In this darkest of plays, the only bright spot is Ophelia's flowers and in her first scene she lightly tosses off a common metaphor: "primrose path." Later, they will drown her. Ophelia is walking a fine line and knows when and how to act. She understands and foils the boys' dirty innuendoes. She is only undone by Hamlet's bizarre and obscene behavior at the play when all the boundaries of truth and artifice are blurred, not the least of which is Hamlet's disturbing and loud role that puts the action in the audience, not the stage. Playing the fool, he shocks Ophelia by revealing their intimacy to anyone who wants to believe it. (Shakespeare is fooling here too, as he puts the customary, obscene and comic "jig" in the middle of the play and makes it part of the action.)

Were Gertrude and Polonius aware of their children's dalliance and did they wink at it? If so they certainly paid for their parental lapses. They are both haunted by the worst anxieties that can beset the parents of teenagers: fears of sexual immorality, addiction, suicide, mental illness and lying.

Ophelia's madness after Hamlet's rejection of her and his murder of her father has a puzzling ambiguity. Has Ophelia really snapped or mastered the teenage art of lying truthfully? Who taught her those bawdy ditties about the maid who was "tumbled", then abandoned? The symbolism in her flowers seems quite sane, a code. Here and throughout, this play blurs all boundaries: truth and untruth, honor and guilt, love and hatred, flesh and corpse, reality and fiction, death and sleep. The only line that rings true through all the murky ambiguity is Hamlet's: "I did love thee once" (III.1.115).

Ophelia's drowning is the most implausible suicide ever written and caps off her brutal neglect. Anyone who could report it in such detail could have easily plucked her out of the water. Gertrude's description of her floating on the water resembles the wedding bed she had hoped to have decked with flowers, not the "sweets" she ended up strewing on Ophelia's grave.

Truth is the central problem of the play and Hamlet's internal struggle to justify a blood feud is the play's drama. If the ghost is truly Hamlet's father then the former king must be avenged. Or is this a demonic vision, sent from the Father of Lies? Hamlet states the dilemma of the play when he first sees his father's ghost:

> Angels and ministers of grace defend us!
> Be thou a spirit of health or goblin damned,
> Bring with thee airs from heaven or blasts from hell,
> Be thy intents wicked or charitable,
> Thou com'st in such a questionable shape
> That I will speak to thee. (I.4.39-44)

If his father was murdered, then the ghost is his father's soul in purgatory. That alone would give the Renaissance audience goose bumps and cause their hair to stand on end. Purgatory was officially illegal in Protestant England, but how else could an injured victim cry out to the next generation? There must have been some who wondered if the play would be closed down for such a controversial topic, before *Hamlet* became firmly established as the most popular of all Shakespeare's plays and "pleasing to all." Hamlet must decide if the ghost is telling the truth. If he is, then the ghost is a "spirit of health" and Hamlet has no choice but to act. But first he must resolve his doubt, which he does with the intricate device of a "play within the play" or as he calls it, *The Mousetrap*.

The drama is not contained in action, but Hamlet's dilemma. Shakespeare modernized an old blood revenge theme by internalizing the conflict and inventing the soliloquy, perhaps an innovation borrowed from Montaigne. Montaigne introduced his essays, hottest new Renaissance genre, by saying that his subject was himself. Hamlet is the subject of *Hamlet*.

Stalling for time, Hamlet goes Goth (or emo) and pretends to be mad. He is disgusted by his mother's midlife sexuality and turns vehemently prudish, probably protesting too much. He bewails his own "too sullied" flesh. He is sternly critical of his uncle's drinking. The role reversals are heavy—the adults are behaving like college students and Hamlet becomes the bonesetter who must put the time back into joint.

Of course he delays. He has to kill his uncle, ruin his mother's reputation and destroy his relationship with Ophelia. He knows there will be no living happily ever after. How easy is it for a "noble heart," a princely young man, to do all that?

So the play becomes the thing. Through artifice, truth will out and it does. Claudius' shock proves the ghost is not a demon and well, then, purgatory exists. In theatre anyway. Is it true religion? Or were these closet beliefs so engrained in English hearts that they had their own verity? In his most memorable acting role Shakespeare himself played the ghost and boldly exhumed this doctrine.

As soon as the players he had sent for arrive, Hamlet becomes excited and starts a lively dialogue with them, reciting lines and demonstrating the differences between good and bad acting. It's fascinating to think we are getting an inside look at rehearsals at the Globe and Shakespeare's directing style. But at the same time, there is a self-hatred here that fights with his excitement: "That I, the son of a dear father murdered, / Prompted to my revenge by heaven and hell, / Must like a whore unpack my heart with words…" (II.2.523-26).

In life we all at times play roles, assume parts. That lies are part of the fabric of our lives is true: "All the world's a stage, / And all the men and women merely players" (*As You Like It,* II.7.138-39). Shakespeare's prodigious output towards the end of his career came with a growing cynicism until we get this comment in *King Lear*: "When we are born, we cry that we are come / To this great stage of fools" (IV.6.180-181). Shakespeare began this theme early in the sonnets and could never leave it alone.

The play presented for the Danish court, *The Murder of Gonzago*, is a tour de force of playwriting. Shakespeare treats us to a much older style, perhaps the kind of outdoor theatre he saw as it passed through Stratford when he was a boy. The lines recited are badly written, too long, on a classical subject and we are just as bored as Polonius. The lines are highly stylized and antique. If Shakespeare is showing off, well, sometimes genius just can't help itself.

Hamlet, the modern man, turns inward. In contrast Fortinbras (Strong In Arm) is relegated to a subplot. He is a man of action who is bent on avenging his father. Fortinbras appears off in the distance, in a shadowy play of ancient and uncomplicated bloodlust. His revenge plot is foiled by the internal strife in Denmark, which he inherits by just walking on stage at the end. It seems inglorious and not quite right, but how else to end this mess?

If Hamlet could turn inward, so could Shakespeare, and he often did not like what he saw. With his success in London Shakespeare was able to repair the social slippage his father had created and assure himself the status of gentleman, complete with a coat of arms. But he was always at odds with his talent and genius; he was jealous of the social elites above him and could get sick to death of play acting. There was something not quite right about it, boys convincingly mimicking women, so much artifice. He called it whoring. A. L. Rowse was spot-on regarding Shakespeare's ambivalence towards his profession. When Shakespeare needed, at times begged Southampton's continued patronage (a certain low in his life) his sonnets reveal that he was to his own self true. "Before this, early on, we find Shakespeare lamenting his lot, expressing his resentment at his ill-fortune, his station and circumstances in life: it is a theme he returns to again and again:

'Wishing me like to one more rich in hope,
Featured like him, like him with friends possessed,
Desiring this man's art, and that man's scope,
With what I most enjoy contented least ...' (29)

That looks like a deprecating reference to his profession as an actor: he must have enjoyed his talent, while resenting the necessity to live by it and the station in life to which it consigned him."[1]

Another scholar, Jonas Barish, wrote about the antitheatrical prejudice in a society that loved to be entertained but condemned the immorality of theatre life and banished it to outside the city proper. The upper class were not only patrons but addicted to play going. In *Coriolanus* Shakespeare uses this character to speechify against acting: "Must I / With my base tongue give to my noble heart / a lie that it must bear?" (III.3.99-101). A few lines later he hates the politician's role even more: "Well, I must do't. / Away, my disposition, and possess me / Some harlot's spirit!" (III.3.110-112).

Besides having to bear society's official contempt for theatre, Shakespeare seems to be personally sickened at times by his obsession. Since these values have been inverted in the twentieth century, it seems quaint to us to have "legitimate" theatre condemned. Even Hollywood freaks are celebrated and so it is odd and painful to hear Shakespeare write about his shame-faced self contempt before the elite gentry. Again Rowse describes how Shakespeare resented the necessity of having to travel about the country as an actor, that he would have preferred to be known as a gentleman and poet. In the Sonnets, which are autobiography throughout, he tells us ruefully,

Alas, 'tis true I have gone here and there,
And made myself a motley to the view;
Gored mine own thoughts, sold cheap what is most dear... [2] (110)

"The next sonnet breaks out with unwonted bitterness:

O, for my sake do you with Fortune chide,
The guilty goddess of my harmful deeds,
That did not better for my life provide,
Than public means which public manners
breeds. (111)

If only he had been born in independent circumstances! No one has ever spoken out more openly what he really felt about his luck in life and his wish that his birth and fortune had been better... . He is branded with the name of a common player, which he is. And he gives a deeper reason for resenting it:

And almost thence my nature is subdued
To what it works in, like the dyer's hand. (111)

That is, he is afraid that acting will affect his own inner nature, cheapen it, make him false—the thing he hated more than anything. All through his writing we find that he is exceedingly conscious of the thin line between 'seeming' and 'being', appearance and reality, falseness and truth. He was the most honest of men.[3]

While most artists are ambivalent about using their personal lives as material, Shakespeare had the additional complication of needing to be obsequious, fawning, even flirtatious with Southampton, a man he genuinely admired, found attractive and who had pained him deeply in a love triangle with a woman. (Probably the Dark Lady they shared of Sonnet 138: "When my love swears that she is made of truth / I do believe her, though I know she lies.") Still, he needed the financial support of Southampton's family during this crisis period. Happily he was able to move on when the plague years ended, the theaters reopened and his most profitable years lay before him. William Shakespeare was compelled to write, direct and act in plays, to hold a spellbound audience in suspended disbelief. He was Prospero.

In *Lear*, Shakespeare bases the entire play on a much more convoluted vision of truth and honesty. Cordelia refuses to tell the truth, that she loves her father, because it would have cast her in the same troupe as her heinous, hypocritical sisters. Her silence drops a depth charge into the family. Lear's neat plan for succession turns into anarchy, foreign war. Scene by scene the play peels back layers of ceremonial civility until the true natures of the children are revealed to their parents and the audience. What is only spoken of in *Hamlet*, plucking at an old man's beard, is executed on stage in *Lear*. Perhaps Goneril and Regan, wicked as they are, were holding together a faulty fabric of government and society with their artificial speeches that pleased their father. The little white lies that smooth ruffled feathers, the words left unsaid—much peace can come from these.

Finally, after trying to find a social defense for artifice, enduring a career that condemned him to a lowly social rank but financially quite well off, Shakespeare retired to Stratford. As Coriolanus says, "For you, the city, thus I turn my back. / There is a world elsewhere" (*Coriolanus*, III.3.136). He did not publish his sonnets or his plays. In Stratford he took up his last role as a gentleman who had made shrewd investments and lived well at New Place with its orchards and improvements. He traveled to London and died unexpectedly at the age of fifty-two from a fever. Was he happy in his last years? This too is silence.

Wonderful Window

In America this great problem (wearing dresses) has been solved, while the fashion lasts, by girls' common adoption of what were formerly masculine work-clothes, i.e. blue denim overalls (called 'blue jeans' or 'dungarees') or some other form of trousers.
—SIMON de BEAUVIOR

When Simone de Beauvoir published that footnote to *The Second Sex*, I was a young girl growing up in Evanston, Illinois. Beauvoir, lifetime companion of Jean Paul Sartre, was living in Paris in their utterly raisonnable and liberated arrangement which allowed both of them to write and pursue infidelities. I had no idea that by wearing blue jeans, running around and riding bikes I was in any way advancing the cause of women. I didn't know women had a cause.

I wore skirts and dresses to school and sensible, brown shoes my mother said would allow my feet to develop healthfully. Otherwise I wore cotton tee shirts and pajamas and Girl Scout uniforms. In the summer we all endured a week of sore and stubbed feet until they developed calluses. Then we ran barefoot all summer, even to ride our bikes—oh, happy days of little traffic and no helmets.

Our backyard in Evanston, Illinois, in 1956. My younger sister and I are both wearing jeans. While I was pondering existentialism, she had her eye on the practical benefits of feminism.

I used to rifle through my older sisters' closets and gaze with amazement as they got ready for dates. They would transform themselves with crinolines and Merry Widow bras into very different creatures than those who shoveled coal into our furnace winter mornings in Pendleton skirts, before racing off to catch the bus to high school. I remember gasping in fear when one of their sorority sisters curled her eyelashes; I thought she was trying to remove her eyeball.

As a teen, I bought what stretch pants and angora sweaters I could afford and waited for the bus in winter on Lake Shore Drive with no hat, de rigueur. In 1966 I spent the summer in Paris and brought home the absolute latest fashions, which my sisters copied. I mean, we all sewed. Recently I sold a crocheted suit I had bought on the Left Bank that caused gasps when I returned home.

It was not until the 1970's that my consciousness was raised and I realized women's clothing was a political issue. Bra burning made brief headlines and Gloria Steinem's exposé of the Playboy Bunny outfit landed her on the Dick Cavett Show. She had the figure for it and wore mini-skirts like a winner. As for me, I have always lived in northern climates and never succumbed again to the ever-returning mini skirt. Besides, in seventh grade I had started wearing uniforms and that began a slow snuffing out of interest in clothing. I still wear a uniform; every day I put on the same Eddie Bauer pants and tops.

The bra burning made me think that maybe women *were* making progress and I was eagerly anticipating the demise of pantyhose. Our "sisters" living on communes had foregone shaving, as the sensible Euro thing to do. But having a job in downtown Chicago, the best I could manage was changing into walking shoes after work.

My first clue that something had gone awry was the

movie *10*. Bo Derek looked sensational, but that movie was about hair. Her beautiful cornrows were new and interesting, but what was with that bathing suit? I mean, where was her other hair? This will never catch on, I thought. Ouch.

I have had decades now to observe, in my haphazard way, women's fashions. Micro-minis were followed by bikini waxing, epidemic bulimia, piercings, tattoos, thongs displayed above low-slung pants exposing midriff baby fat or middle-age stretch marks. I am shocked at how much women are spending on corsets that make the girdle my mother wore seem comfortable. I'm not sure the word "fashion" applies anymore. Could even a Jackie Kennedy lead fashion when a flapper dress from the '20's worn with a bustier and high platform shoes is in style? Styles revolve so quickly that they are now simultaneous.

I tried to understand it. Why give up so much comfort and ease? These are the children whose parents went to Woodstock and Haight Ashbury, the children of neo-pagans, hence... These are the children whose parents tried literally everything so there is a very little frontier of taboo behavior so naturally... (Still, it does make me squeamish when the sandwich artist at Subway can't talk very well because he just got a new bolt in his tongue.)

Having ditched my copy of *The Second Sex* many moves ago, I went to the library to revisit Beauvoir. The county had one copy, but it was lost. Barnes and Noble had one copy in its "Women's Studies" section, but my eye was caught by a shelf one rack over loaded with copies of *Pledged* by Alexandra Robbins. On the cover are three beautiful girls wearing tank tops (no bras but there is something called a ..."shelf"?). Robbins went underground in Greek society on American campuses in the same way Gloria Steinem investigated the exploitation of women by the Playboy Clubs in 1963. Robbins reports rampant drug use, promiscuity, alcoholism, eating disorders, date rape and racism. Worse, these girls want so much to belong that they submissively obey their sorority elders against their own consciences.

Beauvoir's panacea for the oppression of women was the elimination of marriage and universal employment. Well, most women have jobs and marriage is definitely optional. Intellectual autonomy, as Beauvoir predicted, has not evolved universally among "the sex." Beauvoir died six years after Sartre, alcoholic and addicted to amphetamines, constantly quarreling with the bimbo he left all his money to. She's not the only one. So did many matrons in Evanston, Illinois. All I know is I got to avoid a lot of uncomfortable clothing and mutilation, lucky to have been born in a window of time that came after corsets and before tattoos (unless you were in the *National Geographic*). It was a wonderful decade to be a little girl.

Just Go

Children go off in all kinds of ways. The American script is that at eighteen, ready or not, they are drop kicked into college. Some are too old to stay home; some are too young to leave, but that's the plan.

Every family handles it differently. Sometimes the child spends the year acting out: "We had a terrible time with Josh his senior year." Or, "I just want him to go into the military. Let them feed him." I greeted one friend in church and the conversation turned to her eldest daughter, a senior in high school applying to college. My friend accelerated quickly at the thought of this girl, and heatedly described her arrogant, hurtful immaturity. She said she felt like saying to her, "Just go! You know everything, so just go!" Another phrase I hear a lot, with feeling, is: "You want them to go." You do. They are ready. They need to. They become visibly restless. Moody. And you and they are both scared. Sometimes there is a lot of weeping before, during and after. Daily phone calls which hopefully become emails which hopefully taper off to this: "Well, Mom, if you do come, I might be busy."

Some families martial facts proving that for reasons of thrift or tribal tradition the child must attend a local university. Some make a small career of getting their child into a name school and that cachet assuages their loss. I know two mothers who after bravely settling their children into their dorms, went home and lay down on the child's bed in the terribly empty room and sobbed, clinging to the smell that lingered in the sheets.

I try to remember what I was like the year before college. Having an unhappy home life, I couldn't wait to leave. The adults around me seemed to be plodding through immense fatigue, losers, pitiable. They had a perplexing collection of ointments, careers that had peaked a while ago. Their muttering would turn into a shout for no reason at all. I recently told my fifteen-year-old he was "omniscient" and then remembered that my father had used that phrase to describe me often. My own father was counting the years till he would be free of the burden of raising us, retire to the country and go into politics. I couldn't wait to leave high school and get away from these relics. I had bigger fish to fry. I had the world by the tail!

I was shocked on my own second day at college when my father called. I suddenly felt so homesick and little. So scared. Afraid I might cry. I tried to smile while one girl sang lustily all the verses of "Oklahoma" in a fit of bonding euphoria, but I felt so trapped by this foreigner's cheerfulness I wanted to die. I didn't. I adjusted quickly and loved it. Then came the first mixer. What do these kids, so far away from home, Mom and Dad and the environment in which they were raised, do at school? They are so excited. They had been so ready to leave and so scared. Their parents were exasperated and also putting up a brave front because, face it, it was the end of the family as we knew it. The traditional answer to this is that they drink. Not all. Some settle in more soberly, some just flee. But most go to their first kegger, often launching Future Alcoholics of America.

When our older boy was a senior in high school, I found myself waiting at Eddie Bauer's with a return. Standing in line I started thinking that in six weeks he would turn eighteen. What would we get him? Money was tight, so I thought I might pop for getting his muffler fixed. He would have to register with Selective Service. I'd also give him $500 because it's such a big birthday. Then I thought, no, $1500. And a new cell phone. No, a gift certificate so he could pick out any cell phone he wanted. Tears were streaming down my face. "Woman," I said to myself, "you are totally out of control."

Well, at least I'm not alone. Elizabeth Stone summed it up: "Making the decision to have a child—it's momentous. It is to decide forever to have your heart go walking around outside your body."

Carly Simon described how "Love of My Life" came to her when her daughter Sally, eighteen, was about to leave to go to Brown University:

As the youngsters strode to their bedrooms that night, Carly impulsively called out: "You are the love of my life!" The angst of motherhood—both prosaic *and* operatic ("My heart is riding on a runaway train!") illuminated the song. [1]

Even Anna Quindlen realized she was painfully out of a job that had come to be her:

The end result is that the empty nest is emptier than ever before; after all, at its center was a role, a vocation, a nameless something so enormous that a good deal had to be sacrificed for it, whether sleep or self or money or ambition or peace of mind. Those sacrifices—or accommodations, for those of us waxing poetic about their end—became the warp and woof of our lives; first we got used to them and then before we knew it they had become obsolete...Sometimes I go into their rooms and just stand, touching their books, looking out their windows.[2]

The kids all handle it differently. Here's how one father described his daughter's farewell:

Four times, with four kids, we went through it: a friend's car waits in the driveway, and I reluctantly help lug out boxes of her clothes, books, CDs and twisted hangers. I'm thinking, does perky, off-to-college Miss Blue Jeans know how much this is ruffling up her father and mother? Does she realize what I realize, that she will never again be a permanent part of our lives? That she's about to make friends we will never know?[3]

Lucky the parent with a compliant child who does everything the college advisor recommends. Some girls nail down every detail—early admission, job and laundry money settled by fall of their senior year in high school. Not so at our house. Family tensions mounted as deadlines approached and our older boy seemed as unable to act as, well, Hamlet. We swallowed lectures, worried and watched while he dawdled. He applied to two universities and was accepted by both and seemed to never notice our hand wringing.

The teen years cannot be overstated, only overplayed. I could only hope our family room floor would not be littered with corpses come June. So much angst—so much love.

Lonely

O Lord, You have searched me and known me ... / And are acquainted with all my ways.

—PSALM 139:1-3

Ah have no voice. Ah am a Yankee. Okay, not even a real Yankee. Ah cain't write lak Olive Ann Burns or Mark Twain or William Faulkner or Eudora Welty or even Jan Karon. I especially can't make a great deal of money as Frank McCourt did in writing *Angela's Ashes*. That is a book that had huge, compelling voice, even after the story line had wobbled to smut. I was not raised in Ireland but in Chicago and speak with a pitiable twang.

I also read too much. C. S. Lewis famously quoted one of his students as saying, "We read to know we are not alone." Reading connects me with a world of people who don't know me, don't know I should be getting dinner ready and who come from exotic places. There are no books written in a fascinating Chicago dialect because, well, it is considered unlovely. A southern accent can be made to sound stupid, intelligent or sexy. At any rate it bespeaks a different place than the citizenship of news anchors, who are not supposed to have any revealing dialect.

The fact is I am lonely. I grew up in a family of four girls and live with one husband and two sons. I am homesick for the company of women. I know women. I have an instinctual, gender-derived understanding of what other women are up to. That is something I do have.

Unlike Freud, I also know what women want. They want options. They want to have a job or a career—or not. They want to have children—or not. They want to have a husband—or not. They want security and children. Usually. They marry men who want money and sex and pretty soon in the soup of marriage they both end up wanting all four things together. Maybe. Arrangements can be made.

I used to feel sorry for mothers of very young children if they had girls. The girls were born knowing everything. They were shameless flirts at one. At two they knew how to hurt feelings. By three they had a complex grasp of how to push everyone's buttons and by four they had usually gotten some poor little boy to fall in love with them and propose. If they were mad at you, they could play complex psychological games and were masters of manipulation. I just adored my poor stupid little boys who solved most issues by slugging someone or something. They, lambs to slaughter, had no idea why they had just been jilted by little Miss Scarlet O'Hara on the Kindergarten bus. They were so frank, forthright and honest. And at that age, they were pathetically bad at lying.

That was then. Now my boys are teenagers and I am tired of tripping over athletic cups, listening from upstairs to their endless movie soundtracks of glass breaking, guns, cars crashing and women screaming. I long for something a little more civilized. I once stood in my neighbor's house with my jaw dropped looking at her four-year-old daughter's room, which had been organized by her junior high sisters. This child has probably 250 articles of clothing, mostly passed down from her sisters. (I have to admit to a spending spree when she was born on miniature dresses that would shame Imelda Marcos.) It is hard for me to imagine living with people who are *for* civilization, who would, on their own initiative, cuff and roll about twenty-five pairs of socks. (Of course, I know girls who have messy rooms too.)

This summer my fifteen-year-old went on a primitive canoe trip for a week in the Boundary Waters. As I read over the list of items to pack, my brows arched somewhat at the specification of *two* pairs of underpants. What about the other five days? When we, make that I, sorted through the odorous mass that was his stuff-bag upon return, I noticed that only one pair had been used. He explained that after one day you simply turned the pair around and wore them the other way. On the third day you turned them inside out and on the fourth day you repeated the clever rotation of the second day. By the fifth day, I mean, who would care? While he has not a hygiene atom in his brain, he did come back cured of some early adolescent love sickness and seemed his old, happy self. Or his new happy self. He went on to a brilliant career as a Dairy Queen chef, where they made him wash his hands.

Perhaps it is just me, who I am. After sixth grade I began to see the world as a wider place than the Lincoln School. Junior High had lots of kids, new teachers, and I lost my bearings. I had to find my place in Junior High and I did. Then we moved and I lost track again of how I fit in. Then followed long stretches of wonderfully fitting in because no one cared what shaped peg you were. Then longer stretches of feeling that I did not fit in at all and worse, I didn't want to. I often keep my home life and my inner life private so I have "someone" to come back to. Usually we just read, but it's nice. This is a preservation technique I learned in adolescence.

Ronald Blythe writes about retired army officer Colonel Trevor West in *Akenfield: Portrait of an English Village*:

> His ignoring of the local jeremiahs and his indifference to the clan activities of the various social groups in the neighbourhood, plus a certain old-fashioned "distinction" in his personality, sets him rather apart. He is married and has three sons. He is a lonely man, although it isn't Suffolk which has made him so; his

Lonely

is the nature which is alone in any country.[1]

Another author who has considered the penseroso type is Sarah Orne Jewett. In *The Country of the Pointed Firs* she describes a picturesque Maine village, complete with an aged woman who lives alone on an island facing the town on the shore:

There was the world, and here was she with eternity well begun. In the life of each of us, I said to myself, there is a place remote and islanded, and given to endless regret or secret happiness; we are each the uncompanioned hermit and recluse of an hour or a day; we understand our fellows of the cell to whatever age of history they may belong.[2]

Suppose you were a woman born in 1830 in rural New England, were a prolific poetic genius with a caustic wit. It might be a rough go in the sewing circle. Emily Dickinson wrote about her isolation and private rewards:

There is another Loneliness
That many die without—
Not want of friend occasions it
Or circumstance of Lot

But nature, sometimes, sometimes thought
and whoso it befall
Be richer than could be revealed
By mortal numeral — (1138)

No poet has a better friend than Dickinson's biographer, Alfred Habegger, who explains this inner state as it might be interpreted by her "pert" sister Vinnie:

> That is, there exists a rare and rich type of loneliness, one that does not stem from social or other deprivations but rather from native endowment or personal "thought." ... Once, specifying the distinct contribution of each family member, (her sister) wrote that Emily, 'had to think—she was the only one of us who had that to do.'[3]

But it is not well to think too much on the subject of loneliness. You may drift into uncharted water, the bayous called "Solipsism" or "Existentialism." The estuary of "My Spouse Really Doesn't Know Me." As Chekhov warned, "If you are afraid of loneliness, don't get married." You might feel lost, as if trying to find your room in the Alzheimer's ward. Sometimes I think about moving back to Chicago or to California, where most of my family lives. But I can't do it. I've lived in Bloomington, Minnesota, too long and even feel disoriented on Michigan Avenue. My friends are here. I understand why old people have to be pried out of their houses, even if they are lonely. It's better than feeling lost.

Last Christmas our seventeen-year-old talked us into letting him take a girl on a date to a prom, to be responsible for her. He phoned a girl he knew from fishing and canoe trips and who went to our church. She immediately said yes. She is a tomboy who grew up to be a lovely blond and was no small ornament on my son's arm. He did a great deal of driving, corsage buying, dancing, paying for things and then took her home in my van. He returned safe and sound and his dad and I offered hosannas of praise.

The next day I opened the door on the passenger side of my van and noticed that there was glitter on the seat. Something feminine had been there. Maybe, somewhere in my future, if I'm really nice and play my cards right, I could have a friend. A girl. Someone to cook with, someone who might want a gift that is something I've heard of—someone to share this whole process with all over again.

Grief

I finally popped $3.00 at the library for the "Bestseller Express" of Joan Didion's book *The Year of Magical Thinking* (Alfred A. Knopf, 2005). I did it because I had checked the reserve list and I was 310 out of 410 people waiting for the book. People starved for anything not stupid.

The book is about her husband's sudden death in 2003 while she was, simultaneously, dealing with her daughter's cascading health problems (apparently due to a hospital in Manhattan failing to treat pneumonia). It is also about the author trying to understand all of the medical causes and emotional fallout. Since the personal essay is her forte, Didion is nothing if not self-conscious. Why, she asks herself, does she immediately try to learn neuropathology? She describes her own cognitive lapses and the reader can only feel how deeply alone she is. She is not surrounded by other aging sisters or grandchildren to help her out of her mistakes. There is no soothing presence here, mainly friends, doctors, literati...people she needs to appear smart for. There is also the physical shock that begs to be understood. The reader is grateful for her friend who does seem to understand this and brought Didion a quart of ginger flavored Chinese congee every day for weeks. It was all she could eat.

The book is hugely empty. Her husband's absence echoes off the walls of her Manhattan apartment. Her daughter is in ICU most of the time. (While the book doesn't mention it, her daughter's illness ends in death.) Her faith is largely ritual, and she is rightfully angry at its failure. One phrase she is enamored of and repeats is this: "No eye is on the sparrow." There is not the comfort of knowing that her husband, John, is in a better place, that she will meet him again one day. The consolation of I Thessalonians is absent: "Brothers, we do not want you to be ignorant about those who fall asleep, or to grieve like the rest of men, who have no hope."

Sadly lacking too is the intellectual sinew of her earlier work, earlier by thirty-plus years. Joan Didion wrote this book when she was 69 or 70. Her fans aren't getting any younger and we are all interested in how we are going to face the death of a spouse and the empty, empty house. The clothes. But this book suffers from the same problem as her last book, *Where I Was From*. Both have Severe Computer Syndrome. As a journalist and essayist in the '60's and '70's, Didion worked from scraps of paper, quotations and ideas she wrote in a notebook. Then her brain synthesized the fragments into an intense, driving whole as she typed on her beloved Olivetti. *Where I Was From* shows the disarray brought on by too much Cut and Paste. Too much Copy Here, Ctrl C and Ctrl V. *The Year of Magical Thinking* is tied together with about seven leitmotifs, phrases important to her or to her family, and they are supposed to provide structure for her difficult present and many flashbacks. For example, "You're safe. I'm here." is a phrase she uses to reassure her daughter and to ironically underscore her helplessness in the midst of medical trauma.

Didion does not show us her grief in any homely honesty. The picayune minutia she describes—what dishes she puts in the dishwasher and why, the grocery list—are fascinating because you can relate to this miniaturizing of life. If you have ever gone through grief, you know about the quotidian snipers—the place you automatically set at the table for no one, now. But for a book about grief, she hides a lot.

Is grief describable? I've often tried to imagine Dylan Thomas at his father's bedside shouting "Rage, rage against the dying of the light." It's Welsh and all that, but I don't think it is real. I do understand the poem is about his own anger at abandonment.

"Kiddish" is more readable than "Howl," but again it is the anger stage of grief and pretty unique to Ginsburg's tragic childhood. Didion may ignore the horrible nights, but she does a good job with the little things that can totally undo a person: the shoes, the pens.

The Year of Magical Living comments haphazardly on grief literature. C. S. Lewis wrote about his wife's death in *A Grief Observed*. He did not write it for publication and published it under a pseudonym a few years before his death. It is a journal of raw pain and deeply honest. It describes things few people talk about, for example, how embarrassing it is to be bereaved, how he notices a friend cross the street to avoid him. Didion dismisses Lewis' book. He had taken on *The Problem of Pain* much earlier in his life in a book with that title. Clearly Lewis was shocked at how his wife's suffering rocked his faith, at how angry he was at God. He calls God names. Well, so did Job. God can take it.

Didion compares the death of her husband with the deaths of her parents. She was prepared for their deaths at advanced age after increased debility and treats us with a wonderful quote from a letter she received at that time:

> After my mother died I received a letter from a friend in Chicago, a former Maryknoll priest, who precisely intuited what I felt. The death of a parent, he wrote, 'despite our preparation, indeed, despite our age, dislodges things deep in us, sets off reactions that surprise us and that may cut free memories and feelings that we had thought gone to ground long ago. We might, in that indeterminate period they call mourning, be in a submarine, silent on the ocean's bed, aware of the depth charges, now near and now far, buffeting us with recollections.'[1]

In shocking contrast her husband, John Gregory Dunne, died in his early seventies from a massive and sudden heart attack while she was putting dinner on the table—too soon and way too much with their daughter enduring months in ICU. C. S. Lewis opens *A Grief Observed* with this sentence: "No one ever told me that grief felt so much like fear." There are many reasons for this feeling. The loss of a loved one diminishes us; we feel confused and lost. My own mother died when I was eleven and I learned that grief is terrifying because at times you also cease to exist. I might excitedly start to run home with the news that I had been elected class president or shocked that I had been dumped by my best friend, only to realize that *she* was not there to listen, to confirm this reality and so, for a long time, parts of me didn't exist at all. When hastening home with the news that we were named employee of the month, we suddenly remember. We fall into that void and temporarily don't exist.

My mother's death was also embarrassing to me because, in my grammar school class, there were no divorced parents and only one girl's mother worked outside the home; she taught second grade in that building. Rarely did a family even move. This was a bygone era in which Kindergarten teachers wore an old dress to school the first day because there would be so many crying children leaving Mom for the first time. They would hug and console slobbering children. The children learned, as children do, to adjust to this new place, which in our case was a fairyland of stained glass, a wooden bridge over a fish pool, a loft with dollhouses in it, tables and easels.

Reconstruction is slow and can only be done by the bereaved. The loss must be allowed to diminish and new joys found. (If you look closely at the cover, the letters J O H N have a slightly bluish cast. This was a marriage for the record books.) The phrase "that indeterminate period they call mourning" is right. One widower might take years to get his bearings; one might remarry in six weeks.

In her 1967 essay "Goodbye to All That" Didion described how her husband, John, kindly and gently rescues her from clinical homesickness in Manhattan. It was simpler then. They flew back to jasmine scented Los Angeles and lived a happy, mutually devoted and productive twenty-four years. Trying to make sense of her East Coast–West Coast issues, she declared in 1967 that New York was a good city to be young in. Now, bereft, she is surely grateful for her publishers and for the people who come to listen to her readings in the New York City Public Library. For the play Vanessa Redgrave acted in that was made out of her book.

Didion once defined a writer as a person "whose most absorbed and passionate hours are spent arranging words on pieces of paper." Writing is one way she tries to deal with the awful losses, recover the grieving she couldn't do as she focused on her daughter. Discussing the book in an interview with Rachel Donadio, Didion said that she started writing and organizing her notes as a way to grieve: "the only way I understand anything is to write it down." That she hides a lot is pure Didion. It is part of her commitment to beauty.

This Happy Isle

Call this a footnote, but has anyone been paying attention to British literature for the last four hundred years? Has anyone noticed that they are constantly making up fantasy lands to live in? If you have escaped the cinematic obsession with *Lord of the Rings* or the *Chronicles of Narnia*, you are working harder at it than I am. Somehow, they step through some furniture and are off.

Think about it. In *Coriolanus* Shakespeare writes, "There is a world elsewhere" (III. 3.136). He could easily have been talking about himself, a young man who shook off a wife and three children in his early twenties to go to London to seek fame and fortune. Shakespeare became a wealthy man by Stratford standards in his thirties and achieved fame beyond his wildest dreams.

Maybe Merry Old England wasn't that much fun. Maybe it was wrought with civil wars, famine, foreign aggression, plague, guilt and religious persecution. Maybe? Of course it was. And not just a little. What to do for escape? Well, pagan village rites are fun, but infrequent. That leaves storytelling the national gift. When tired of histories and tragedies, Shakespeare would invent little islands where all kinds of mistaken identities, twin stories and gender bending went on: Illyria in *Twelfth Night*, the uninhabited island in *The Tempest*— imaginary Bermudas. Escape from law and order, such as Athens in *A Midsummer Night's Dream*, could happen in any magical "wood." Even real place names such as Arden or Ephesus seem mythical settings.

Winnie the Pooh had his magical woods. *Wind in the Willows* comes complete with a map of an imaginary country that includes a magical mystery place called Pan Island. I'm not talking about parents who conveniently die so that an adolescent can have a coming of age adventure. I'm talking about grown-ups who invent Never Never Land and Wonderland.

It's fine with me. I need all the books I can get my hands on. Emily Dickinson was forbidden to read for eight months to allow an eye infection to clear up. She didn't like it. "It was a shutting out of all the dearest ones of time, the strongest friends of the soul— BOOKS."[1] And having spent my entire life reading and talking to myself, I can only agree with Logan Pearsall Smith: "People say that life is the thing, but I prefer reading!"

Acknowledgments

We live in a golden age of biography. Not only have the biographies of the founding fathers been pushed to the top of best-seller lists, but biographies of Shakespeare pile up on front tables in airport bookstores.

Some are fun and speculative, but fill in gaps. They are based on what evidence there is from his sonnets, comments made by contemporaries, archeological finds and public record. *Will in the World* by Stephen Greenblatt is fascinating. *A Year In the Life of William Shakespeare* by James Shapiro opens up a world of political comment by paralleling the war in Ireland with war in Hamlet and other contemporaneous events. *Hamlet in Purgatory,* by Greenblatt again, is a must read for anyone interested in this play or the admittedly unknowable religious beliefs of Shakespeare's family. And I am indebted to Joel Fineman for *Shakespeare's Perjured Eye*.

The scholarly advantage, however, goes to A. L. Rowse. He was so deeply read in Elizabethan history and literature as to be almost bicultural and bilingual. His *Shakespeare's Sonnets*, a bracing read, opened my eyes years ago to the biography behind the sonnet sequence, a roman à clef of sorts. The sonnets are, as Rowse points out, Shakespeare's most personal work. *Shakespeare the Man* is highly empathic and thorough, a true source for any scholar.

Shakespeare left no paper trail: no letters, diaries, journals. That scholars respect what little is left and take it as a challenge to dig into the journals of astrologists, explore his lodgings, examine piles of miniatures, etc. testifies to just how fascinating he remains. References such as the names of Emilia, Emilius, Bassianus and Bassanio in his plays would have been understood by many in the audience, but are lost on us without the work of these literary archeologists.

I am forever grateful to my husband for following the fits and starts of my muse and my neighbor Lila who said, "Why don't you write?"

Notes

Jeremy At Bat

[1] George Will, *Bunts* (New York: Scribner, 1998), 192.

[2] Ibid., 38.

I Feel Pretty

[1] Leo Tolstoy, *War and Peace* (New York: Penguin Group, 1968), 547.

[2] R. Wise, (Director). (1961). *West Side Story* (Videotape). Metro-Goldwyn-Mayer Inc.

[3] V. Minnelli, (Director). (1944). *Meet Me in St. Louis* (Videotape). Loew's Incorporated. Metro-Goldwyn-Mayer Inc.

Homeschooling For Dummies

[1] National Home Education Research Institute (database online), Brian D. Ray, Ph.D. (2 July 2008, accessed 13 November 2008); available from http://www.nheri.org/Research-Facts-on-Homeschooling.html; Internet.

[2] Leo Tolstoy, *Anna Karenina* (New York: New American Library, 1964), 528.

Doubt Truth To Be A Liar

[1] A. L. Rowse, *Shakespeare The Man* (New York: St. Martin's Press, 1988), 61.

[2] Ibid., 38.

[3] Ibid., 102-103.

Just Go

[1] Sheila Weller, *Girls Like Us* (New York: Atria, 2008), 516.

[2] Anna Quindlen, "Flown Away, Left Behind," *Newsweek*, 12 January 2004, 64.

[3] Allen R. Sandvik, "A Home's Quiet Sound of Accomplishment Roars," Star Tribune, publication date unknown, HG3.

Lonely
[1] R. Blythe, *Akenfield* (New York: Random House, Inc., 1969), 191.
[2] S. O. Jewett, *The Country of the Pointed Firs* (New York: Modern Library, 1995), 87.
[3] A. H. Habegger, *My Wars Are Laid Away in Books* (New York: Random House, Inc., 2001), 500.

Grief
[1] Joan Didion, *The Year of Magical Thinking* (New York, Alfred A. Knopf, 2005), 27.

This Happy Isle
[1] A. H. Habegger, *My Wars Are Laid Away in Books* (New York: Random House, Inc., 2001), 484.

Portions of "Jeremy at Bat" originally appeared in the *Star Tribune*, May 29, 2004.

Portions of "Just Go" originally appeared in *Rescue Magazine*, June/July, 2004.